Healing from the
Emotionally Absent Mother

Healing
from the
Emotionally Absent Mother

*A Guided Journal to Process Your
Emotions and Build Self-Compassion*

Christy Lincoln, LCPC

ROCKRIDGE
PRESS

Art Direction: Tricia Jang
Interior and Cover Designer: Kristina Spencer
Art Producer: Janice Ackerman
Editor: Adrian Potts
Production Editor: Jael Fogle
Production Manager: Riley Hoffman

Illustration © West Wind Creative/Creative Market

Paperback ISBN: 978-1-63878-332-9
R0

*I have always believed,
and I still believe,
that whatever good
or bad fortune may
come our way we can
always give it meaning
and transform it into
something of value.*

—HERMANN HESSE

Contents

Introduction

Welcome! I am honored to be part of your healing journey. Examining your past to transform your present takes a lot of courage, and I congratulate you on your decision to grow and heal.

I have taken a similar journey. I grew up in what seemed, to the outside world, a loving family. Like all families, we had our struggles, which I thought were just a normal part of any home life. But when I started studying psychology, I realized that some of the dynamics in my family were not ideal for children to feel secure or be their most authentic selves and live a fulfilling life. This discovery was like water in the desert for me. I set out to learn more, and along the way I found my life's passion. I became a therapist over twenty years ago and have been privileged to work with many clients facing similar issues.

Growing up with an emotionally absent mother is a recognized source of ongoing issues into adulthood. But there is good news: acknowledging and addressing the harm can help people work through their past challenges and heal.

Emotional neglect is hard to put your finger on. For some, it can take time to recognize the patterns that occurred in their childhood. Unlike child abuse, an active form of harm,

neglect is passive, a form of omission, and consequently sometimes viewed as less harmful. But the truth is, both neglect and abuse threaten the health, safety, and development of a child in many ways. It is true that abuse and neglect often go hand in hand. However, if your mother was not abusive but neglectful, that can nevertheless have a big impact on your life now.

While I use the word "mother" in this journal, this does not necessarily refer to the woman who gave birth to you. Rather, it can refer to any adult who was your primary caregiver—the person whose role it was to care for, nurture, and protect you as a child. If you were raised by another caregiver, you can still use the prompts and exercises here.

Before we continue, I want you to take a moment to imagine your life and your relationships transformed into something better than you have dared to imagine. This journal is designed to help you heal and move forward toward that better time. Today you begin breaking the patterns of your past and stepping into the future that you want. Please be kind to yourself along the way.

How to Use This Journal

The book is organized into six sections that mirror the progression of the healing journey of my clients. You should feel free to progress at your own pace. You may find there are times when you feel motivated and times when you do not. Trust in your ability to stop when you need to and to forge ahead when you are ready.

The prompts and exercises ahead will help you develop a deeper understanding of the role that your mother has played in your life. Thoughtfully completing the pages will help you make sense of your relationships with your mother, yourself, and others in your life. The reflection and intention that come with writing down your thoughts will be rewarded with growth and healing.

Journaling is a powerful aid for healing. I often encourage my clients to keep a journal and write in it outside of sessions. There's tremendous value in keeping a record of one's complicated, sometimes messy, healing journey. That said, these pages are not intended as a substitute for professional help from a licensed therapist or counselor. If you are struggling with chronic or debilitating emotions related to, or separate from, your mother's neglect or emotional detachment, I encourage you to reach out for help. The Resources list on page 138 is a good place to start. Know that seeking help is a sign of courage and strength.

I have been privileged to walk this journey with many clients over the years, and the contents of this journal encompass the most powerful tools I have used to help them heal. I am grateful for the chance to share them here to help you get to a better place.

The journey of a thousand miles begins with a single step.

—LAO TZU

Unpacking What You Needed from Your Mother

Children need unconditional love, patience, discipline, attention, and consistency to feel secure. They need to know they are their mother's top priority. If you did not get that from your mother, the effects likely first appeared at a young age and have stayed with you to this day.

How we are put together, how we view ourselves, our self-esteem, and the unconscious beliefs we hold about relationships . . . all these things are strongly imprinted on us by our mother. In the case of an emotionally absent mother, that emotional omission can lead to feelings of low self-esteem, anxiety, depression, and other negative emotions.

In the following pages you will explore what your emotional needs were when you were young, how they were neglected, and how this affects you today. This will likely bring up some difficult feelings and memories, so be kind to yourself and feel free to move forward at your own pace.

Take a moment to reflect on why you were drawn to this book. What do you hope to learn about yourself? About your mother? About the relationships in your life today?

_____

_____

_____

_____

_____

_____

_____

_____

_____

_____

_____

_____

_____

_____

_____

Write what you know of your mother's story, outlining the major life events and stressors that you know about. What did your mother want out of life? Was her childhood happy? What was life like for her as a mother of a young child?

_____

_____

_____

_____

_____

_____

_____

_____

_____

_____

_____

_____

_____

_____

Emotional distance is harmful even when it's not the mother's fault. Life events, like poverty, physical or mental illness, or a custody battle, impact the entire family and can inhibit emotional connection. Here, allow yourself to write about what you know or imagine were the reasons behind your mother's emotional distance.

_____

_____

_____

_____

_____

_____

_____

_____

_____

_____

_____

_____

_____

_____

Reflect on what it felt like to be around your mother as a child. Were you anxious, guarded, longing, angry? What did it feel like to be in her presence?

Reconnect with Yourself as a Child

For this exercise, gather some photos of yourself as a child. If you don't have any, search online for images that remind you of childhood, perhaps photos of a pet resembling one you grew up with, or vintage images of a house resembling your childhood home. My clients have used pictures of the neighborhoods they grew up in and the schools they attended. Collect these memories into a scrapbook you create, either digital or physical. While doing this, be kind to yourself. Allow yourself to remember your childhood, and allow yourself to grieve. After gathering the photos, how do you feel? Did any of your feelings surprise you?

_____

_____

_____

_____

_____

_____

_____

_____

_____

_____

_____

_____

_____

_____

Signs of Emotional Neglect

An emotionally distant parent may be able to provide for physical needs, such as food, clothing, and shelter, but remains detached from their child's emotional needs. This is otherwise known as childhood emotional neglect. It can appear in different ways, most notably by not noticing what their child feels, asking about their feelings, connecting with them on an emotional level, comforting them in times of distress, or validating their feelings. When looking back at childhood, it can be difficult at first to distinguish between a common parental shortcoming and emotional neglect. To help you sort through this, check any of the boxes below that you can relate to.

☐ I often felt more like my mother's friend, not her child.

☐ I often felt lonely, or like I didn't belong anywhere.

☐ It seemed like I worried about my mother more than she worried about me.

☐ I felt like I wasn't important to my mother.

☐ I often worried that I was a burden to my mother.

☐ I was hesitant to share my true feelings with my mother.

☐ I tended to keep my problems to myself, rather than share them with my mother.

☐ I was afraid of upsetting or angering my mother.

☐ I rarely felt like my mother truly saw me.

☐ I often wished my mother could be more like the warm mothers I saw on TV shows or in movies.

These are all signs of having experienced some form of emotional neglect. If you are using this journal, it's likely that you checked a number of these boxes. Even if you didn't, the statements above may bring to mind other ways that you experienced neglect. No matter how you responded, what's important is to recognize the patterns of neglect you experienced so that you can start your healing journey.

Allow yourself to feel whatever you are feeling after completing the previous exercise. You may want to disengage from this journal for a while, and that's okay. Take the time you need. When you're ready, it can be beneficial to check in with yourself about what the exercise brought up. Write about the emotions that came up for you. If you are feeling overwhelmed, it may help to try "A Meditation for Self-Care" (page 53) or "Self-Love Affirmations" (page 84).

I am deserving and capable of healing.

Tuning in to Self-Talk

Self-talk refers to the inner voice inside our heads. It's the chatter we say to ourselves and the narrative we create to put our experiences in context. Many of my clients who experienced emotional neglect have told me that their self-talk is quite harsh and judgmental. Check the beliefs below that you relate to. You can add your own beliefs, too.

☐ I am a failure.

☐ Once people get to know me, they won't like me.

☐ I'm so damaged that there is no point in trying.

☐ I will never [find a partner, get a good job, have lots of friends, get what I want].

☐ I am unattractive.

☐ I am worthless.

If you checked any of the boxes on the previous page or added similar thoughts of your own, can you remember when these beliefs first appeared? Were you able to express any of these with your mother as a child? How would you feel about talking this way to a friend or loved one?

_____

_____

_____

_____

_____

_____

_____

_____

_____

_____

_____

_____

_____

_____

_____

Compared to your usual self-talk, how would you like your self-talk to sound? What about a year from now? Ten years from now? At the end of your life? How would your experience in life be different if you spoke to yourself with more care and compassion?

_____

_____

_____

_____

_____

_____

_____

_____

_____

_____

_____

_____

_____

_____

Is there a person in your life, or a favorite fictional character, whom you see as an emotionally present and supportive person? What characteristics or traits do they have that make you think they are emotionally present?

_____

_____

_____

_____

_____

_____

_____

_____

_____

_____

_____

_____

_____

_____

_____

_____

Imagine a time when you've felt very emotionally supported. Write about the circumstances that led to you feeling supported. How did it feel to receive that support?

_____

_____

_____

_____

_____

_____

_____

_____

_____

_____

_____

_____

_____

_____

_____

Reflect on the person who supported you in your previous response. What do you value or admire about them? Write down a few important things that you know about that person.

How does the emotional support you reflected on in the last two prompts compare to what your mother did or did not provide for you as a child? What do you wish she had been able to provide but could not?

How did your mother respond when you expressed your feelings as a child? What happened when you showed strong emotions, such as anger, sadness, or worry? What did this teach you?

_____

_____

_____

_____

_____

_____

_____

_____

_____

_____

_____

_____

_____

_____

In a healthy mother-child relationship, the mother provides unconditional love and emotional support so the child can focus on learning and growing. However, when this is unavailable or inconsistent, the child is left to look after their own emotional needs—and sometimes those of their mother, too. Use the space below to explore how this may have been true for you growing up.

Connect with Your Younger Self

Visualizing yourself as a child can help you get in touch with what you went through and provide the comfort and support you deserved then but didn't have. This can be a challenging practice, so feel free to come back to it later if it seems overwhelming. Or try it with the support of a loved one or a therapist.

1. Sit comfortably and relax into your chair. Take some deep breaths and close your eyes.

2. Imagine yourself as a child when you were hurt, angry, or neglected but did not receive help. What are you thinking or feeling? What do you look like? Where are you?

3. Reflect on what you are feeling, what you want, and what you need in this moment.

4. Now approach the child you're envisioning and ask them how they're feeling. Consider what you would like to say to that child. Offer any compassion, comfort, and encouragement that comes to mind.

5. Complete the practice by saying to the child, "I'm sorry you had to go through that alone, but I love you and I am with you now."

How did this exercise feel? Speaking to your younger self as an adult will help you create a new narrative around your earlier experiences. You can make better sense of what may have seemed confusing at the time, let yourself know you were not to blame, and practice seeing yourself more compassionately.

Did your mother offer gifts or special activities (like bedtime stories, one-on-one time, or promised trips) that never materialized? If you can remember an unmet promise, write about it. How could you do something now for yourself, to show yourself love and respect?

_____

_____

_____

_____

_____

_____

_____

_____

_____

_____

_____

_____

_____

_____

_____

How do you feel about Mother's Day? Many clients have told me that Hallmark does not make cards for the way they feel about their mothers. If you could create an honest Mother's Day card, what would it say? What would you like to feel on future Mother's Days after you have healed?

_____

_____

_____

_____

_____

_____

_____

_____

_____

_____

_____

_____

_____

_____

The best way out is
always through.

—ROBERT FROST

The Legacy of an Emotionally Absent Mother

Our mothers are our first window to the world. With an emotionally available mother, growing up in her loving embrace gives children the courage to explore. Successful parenting doesn't require perfection, though. The influential psychotherapist Donald Winnicott gave us the concept of the "good enough" mother. She doesn't have to be perfect, just good enough. Meaning that whatever her mistakes (we all make them), her child's basic needs are met: not only food and shelter but the emotional needs of love, warmth, and protection.

What happens when we grow up with a mother who falls short? This part of your journal will help you come to terms with what a childhood that lacked "good enough mothering" has done to you and to your relationships as an adult. Be kind to yourself while working on the exercises. Rest assured, many of my clients have come through this journey and now find themselves in a better place. We can't go back and change the past, but we can write a new future: one that includes peace and joy.

Most parent-child relationships fall under what is called a *secure attachment style*. When a child feels comforted by the presence and attention of their mother, they learn that their emotions will be recognized, that they will be supported and loved, and that people, in general, can be trusted. In adulthood, this translates into a healthy self-esteem and a tendency to form healthy relationships. Without this secure attachment, a child can become stressed and struggle to make sense of the world and cope with life's challenges.

Think back to your childhood. Do you remember feeling any confusion about your place in your family, or in the world? Did you often experience stress? Did you feel supported or secure during difficult times? Feel free to write about the good and the bad—whatever comes to mind.

_____

_____

_____

_____

_____

_____

_____

_____

_____

_____

_____

_____

If you grew up with an emotionally absent mother, you likely lacked a secure base from which to explore the world, make sense of your emotions, and form bonds with others. This can lead to *insecure attachment styles* as an adult, which we'll explore in upcoming prompts. You may identify with one or with elements of different attachment styles.

How did your relationship with your mother develop over the course of your childhood? What feelings do you have about your early relationship with her? Was she emotionally available on occasion but distant at other times? Is it difficult to remember her holding you lovingly, smiling, and expressing affection? How did she respond when you were upset or needed help?

People with *anxious attachment styles* are exactly that: anxious about their relationships. If you received inconsistent emotional care from your mother, you became fearful that your needs would not be met, which can ignite an instinct to cling closer to your mother in an attempt to be seen and cared for.

This can affect relationships into adulthood. Have you ever found yourself constantly texting or calling your partner? Do you fear people will leave you easily? Do you get jealous with no evidence? These are some traits of an anxious attachment style. Do you feel you have some of these or similar traits? Record your thoughts below.

Some children whose emotional needs are not met, rather than trying to gain their mother's attention, come to believe it is futile to seek help. They learn to suppress outward displays of emotion and avoid seeking closeness with caregivers. This forms an *avoidant attachment style*, which in adulthood translates as a tendency to wall yourself off from intimacy. It seems too painful to be vulnerable and risk getting rejected again.

Do you tend to be very self-reliant, downplay the importance of close relationships, or feel uncomfortable with emotions—your own or those expressed by others? These are some traits of an avoidant attachment style. Do you feel you have some of these or similar traits? Record your thoughts below.

A *disorganized attachment style* can develop in a child when the person meant to protect them is instead a source of danger. Perhaps your mother was abusive or did not protect you from abuse. As an adult you may go back and forth between wanting to connect with others and wanting to protect yourself. You may feel fear and anxiety when starting a relationship and tell yourself it will never work out. Your self-talk can be harsh and unrelenting. You long for connection, but because fear is intertwined with that longing, you find yourself acting erratically, which requires a very patient partner if the relationship is to last. Do you feel you have some of these or similar traits? Record your thoughts below.

_____

_____

_____

_____

_____

_____

_____

_____

_____

_____

_____

Upon learning more about attachment styles, you may feel sadness, grief, or anger as you reflect on how early experiences with your mother affect you now. That is normal. Most children of emotionally unavailable mothers find themselves in some way exhausted, overwhelmed, guilty, ashamed, doubting themselves, and full of self-loathing. Children are programmed to believe that their caretakers can meet their needs—it's a matter of survival. So rather than blaming the parent when these needs are not met, children often feel guilty and ashamed of themselves.

Choose one or more of these emotions and write about your experience with them up to this point in your life.

Take some time to reflect on how gaining new insight into your early experiences can help you release any confusion, shame, or self-blame you may have carried over the years. What would it feel like to be more forgiving to yourself, knowing that as a child you adapted in the best way you could to circumstances that were beyond your control?

_____

_____

_____

_____

_____

_____

_____

_____

_____

_____

_____

_____

_____

_____

Coping Day to Day

Over the years, my clients have shared many of their coping mechanisms. When pain is hard to bear, people turn to different things. This exercise will help you think about what you do to cope. Some coping methods that you use may be healthy responses to challenges. Think of what you do when faced with challenges or stress, and circle how often you engage in these behaviors.

Go for a walk or be active:	RARELY	SOMETIMES	OFTEN
Meditate or do yoga:	RARELY	SOMETIMES	OFTEN
Ask for help:	RARELY	SOMETIMES	OFTEN
Paint, draw, or color:	RARELY	SOMETIMES	OFTEN
Spend time with my pet:	RARELY	SOMETIMES	OFTEN
Hang out with friends:	RARELY	SOMETIMES	OFTEN
Spend time in nature:	RARELY	SOMETIMES	OFTEN
Read a book:	RARELY	SOMETIMES	OFTEN
Listen to music:	RARELY	SOMETIMES	OFTEN

EXERCISE CONTINUED →

There may be other times you try to cope in ways that might help you feel better in the moment but in the long-term cause you harm. Circle how often you engage in these behaviors.

Isolate from others:	RARELY	SOMETIMES	OFTEN
Watch TV excessively:	RARELY	SOMETIMES	OFTEN
Overexercise:	RARELY	SOMETIMES	OFTEN
Overeat or restrict my eating:	RARELY	SOMETIMES	OFTEN
Use alcohol or drugs:	RARELY	SOMETIMES	OFTEN
Oversleep:	RARELY	SOMETIMES	OFTEN
Go online or use social media excessively:	RARELY	SOMETIMES	OFTEN
Avoid important tasks or issues:	RARELY	SOMETIMES	OFTEN

Give yourself grace as you complete this exercise. You are doing the best you can! Identifying unhealthy coping mechanisms is an important first step in healing. In the next section we will explore self-care practices to replace damaging ones.

I cannot change
the past, but I can
change the future.

Knowing Your Emotions

Growing up in a home in which a range of emotions were not freely expressed, and with a mother who did not help you communicate or manage your feelings, you likely formed an uneasy relationship with your own emotions. Check the boxes you can relate to:

☐ Emotions make me uncomfortable.

☐ I have a hard time trusting people.

☐ "Trust but verify" is my motto.

☐ I find it hard to be truly emotionally open with friends and loved ones.

☐ I find it hard to know what I am feeling most of the time.

Are there certain emotions you can tolerate better than others? Do certain emotions cause you to shut down? Write about your relationship with strong emotions, like anger, fear, frustration, jealousy, or others that come up for you.

_____

_____

_____

_____

_____

_____

_____

_____

_____

Often when a mother is neglectful of the emotional needs of a child, other people, including family members, are not aware of the damage. This can cause feelings of loneliness and isolation. Have you told another person about challenging childhood experiences and not been believed? Or had your story minimized with responses like "But she loves you," "It wasn't that bad," or "You are being dramatic"? How did it make you feel? What do you wish someone had said instead? If you have never spoken to anyone else about what happened to you, reflect below on any isolation you may have felt and how you would like to be supported by others.

Mothering Myself

Often people who were neglected in childhood struggle to take good care of themselves as adults. This exercise will direct your attention to self-care practices that you may be neglecting. Answer the following:

I prepare and eat healthy meals:	RARELY	SOMETIMES	OFTEN
I find time for exercise:	RARELY	SOMETIMES	OFTEN
I prioritize good sleep habits:	RARELY	SOMETIMES	OFTEN
My living space is clean and organized:	RARELY	SOMETIMES	OFTEN
I purchase and wear well-fitting clothes and shoes:	RARELY	SOMETIMES	OFTEN
I practice good grooming habits:	RARELY	SOMETIMES	OFTEN
I regularly visit the doctor and dentist for checkups and appointments:	RARELY	SOMETIMES	OFTEN
I reach out for help when I need it:	RARELY	SOMETIMES	OFTEN
I am kind to myself:	RARELY	SOMETIMES	OFTEN
I forgive myself for my mistakes:	RARELY	SOMETIMES	OFTEN

How did it feel to complete this exercise? How many of these activities should be "often" for you, instead of "sometimes" or "rarely"? Which areas would you like to improve? Are there other things you can do to better look after yourself? Remember, it's never too late to start mothering yourself!

What are holidays and family get-togethers like for you? Do you do all the traveling? Do you spend lots of time looking for the perfect gift for your mother? Do visits leave you feeling sad, worn down, or numb? If your mother has passed away, do the holidays stir up unhappy memories?

_____

_____

_____

_____

_____

_____

_____

_____

_____

_____

_____

_____

_____

What is one positive change you could make in your typical holiday plans? For example, if you return to your hometown, perhaps getting together with old friends once or twice would feed your soul. You might like to stay in a hotel instead of staying with family. If your mother has passed, how might you spend time with loved ones or engage in healthy coping strategies (page 31) to help you through the holidays?

Shame can play a central role in the lives of emotionally neglected children. Self-criticism may have been your younger self's attempt to construct an internal parent to keep you safe. Carried over into adulthood, this shame can feel overwhelming and all-consuming. Do you worry that people would not like you if they saw the real you? Do you believe you are somehow defective deep down? Do you often feel that you let yourself down? How can you feel compassion for your younger self, who had to create their own parent at an early age?

"Need" can be a complicated word for children of emotionally absent mothers, bringing up painful memories of needs not being met. In what ways were you taught that your needs were a burden? Do you sometimes find it difficult to advocate for yourself or ask for help as an adult?

_____

_____

_____

_____

_____

_____

_____

_____

_____

_____

_____

_____

_____

_____

You may have spent so long ignoring your needs that it's hard to identify what they are. Give yourself permission to focus on your needs for a moment. Write down your needs in the following areas of your life.

My health: _____

_____

My time: _____

_____

My family: _____

_____

My relationships: _____

_____

My career: _____

_____

My finances: _____

_____

My spiritual life: _____

_____

Some who suffer emotional neglect become perfectionists, going to great lengths to conform to what they believe their caregiver wants. In adulthood, seeking perfection can give us a sense of control and even help us achieve goals. Ultimately, however, this attitude sets impossibly high standards for us and leaves us reliant on validation from others. In section 4, we'll explore healthy ways to build self-worth. But, for the moment, reflect on how perfectionism may have played a part in your life. Has it helped you in some ways? Does it hold you back in other ways? What would you do in life if you weren't afraid to fail?

Looking at your past can be difficult at times. It is important to take breaks. How do your body and mind let you know you need a break?

_____

_____

_____

_____

_____

_____

What are some ways you can renew your body and mind when you need to? Before moving on to the next section of this journal, list some pleasurable activities you enjoy. Pick one of the activities to do today or in the coming week, and make time for it in your schedule.

_____

_____

_____

_____

_____

_____

Caring for myself is not self-indulgence, it is self-preservation.

—AUDRE LORDE

Section 3
Making Self-Care Your Priority

Many children of emotionally absent mothers spend their childhoods, and often their adulthoods, trying to win their mother's love instead of focusing on themselves. Or perhaps they gave up on finding that love from her but came to believe that they are not worthy of receiving that care from anyone, least of all themselves.

Self-care is an integral step toward healing these damaging beliefs. Prioritizing your own care doesn't mean doing what you want to do all the time, and it doesn't mean ignoring the needs of others. Only after we take care of ourselves can we care for other people.

There are six types of self-care: physical, emotional, social, practical, mental, and spiritual. All are important. As you complete the following exercises and prompts, see whether you can focus on overcoming negative thinking, being nonjudgmental, and letting go of self-criticism. Consider all you have to offer the world, and lean in to taking better care of yourself.

Think about how a lack of emotional support has discouraged you from honoring your own needs. Write about an aspect, or several aspects, of your self-care that you've been discouraged from prioritizing, and the effect that it has had on you.

_____

_____

_____

_____

_____

_____

_____

_____

_____

_____

_____

_____

_____

_____

_____

_____

Often, emotionally absent mothers are not able to model good habits of self-care for their children. Think about your current habits around sleep, hydration, diet, hygiene, and exercise. Write about your ideal health and exercise regimen: How much sleep every night? How much exercise, and what kind? Where did you learn about healthy self-care? Write about what's stopping you from meeting your health ideals.

When was the last time you went to the doctor for a checkup? Are you overdue for a screening or for a dental exam? Do you know what medical care is due for your age and your special health conditions? Write about what care you think you need to stay your healthiest; do some research if you need to. Think about scheduling a basic annual checkup with a doctor and a dentist.

Our parents, especially our mothers, create our first safe and soothing spaces. Emotionally absent mothers often are not able to anticipate and meet the physical needs of their children. What creature comforts do you remember seeking as a child? Was your home unclean, or very sparse? Was the temperature comfortable? Describe what you can remember.

_____

_____

_____

_____

_____

_____

_____

_____

_____

_____

_____

_____

_____

_____

_____

_____

Think back to the first time you had control of your own environment: your first apartment, house, or dorm room. What were the must-have items for that room? Comfy blankets? Houseplants? A really great pillow? Video games? Books? What does that tell you about the things that you really love in a space, like favoring organization or comfort, or displaying items such as souvenirs or diplomas?

Loving My Space

Look around your living space. Do you see anything you love? Anything you don't like or feel ashamed of? This exercise will help you think about what you would like to change, no matter whether you live in a tiny room or a huge house. Check the boxes for changes you would like to make:

☐ Hanging pictures or photographs of things I love.

☐ Cleaning an area that I usually neglect.

☐ Bringing in healthy, vibrant plants to brighten my space.

☐ Getting rid of items that no longer serve me.

Add your own ideas below.

☐ Adding new paint. This can be a wall or the whole house.

☐ Tackling a project I have been putting off.

☐ Adding a pet. This can be a fish or a dog or anything in between.

_____

_____

_____

_____

_____

_____

_____

Our parents shape our palate and provide us with the foods we eat. Some parents don't provide what their children enjoy; some struggle to provide any food at all. Do you have memories around food, either good or bad?

Write about your favorite foods, from chocolate cake to a juicy steak or a candy bar. What are your dream meal and your comfort food snack? Do you keep those things on hand? Do you ever take yourself out to eat at your favorite restaurants? What little or big thing could you do to create better memories around food?

A Meditation for Self-Care

An important part of self-care is to experience a full range of feelings, even challenging ones we would rather avoid. Meditation is a wonderful way to observe your feelings and allow them to come and go rather than avoiding or fighting them. Even a few minutes of meditation a day can help promote self-compassion, invite mindful calm, and develop resilience to the difficulties that we encounter in everyday life. Here's a basic method you can follow:

1. Find a comfortable position and sit quietly. Close your eyes and focus attention on your breathing, feeling the sensations of your inhales and exhales.

2. Slowly inhale for a count of four, hold your breath for a count of four, and exhale for a count of four.

3. As you continue this breathing pattern, consider any uncomfortable feelings you have experienced recently. They could include shame, fear, rejection, or something else.

4. When you encounter this emotion, kindly remind yourself that your feelings are valid and that it is okay to honor them with compassion. Allow the emotion to drift away without judging it.

5. Continue for two minutes or so. When you are ready, take a deep breath and open your eyes.

   Take a minute afterward to reflect on how you felt during and after the meditation.

What did you imagine you would be when you grew up? A football player? A dinosaur researcher? A gymnast? What did you end up doing? Our early career ambitions are often reflections of our first loves. Write about the dream jobs you have idealized in your life and how they differ from what you do now. Think about some of the aspects of those early career dreams, and imagine how you could honor them today, watching a football game or going to a natural history museum, for example.

What brings you joy in your spare time? If you had three days to do anything you want, what would you do? Watch your favorite movies? Plant a flower garden? Build an engine? Write about a pastime that you could engage in for days on end and what it is about that pastime that really excites you.

_____

_____

_____

_____

_____

_____

What if you had just three free hours? Are there any parts of that pastime that you could explore? What if you only had thirty minutes?

_____

_____

_____

_____

_____

_____

_____

Think about someone who made you feel loved. Was there a time when they gave you a gift or something tangible that evoked that feeling? What was it? How did it make you feel?

_____

_____

_____

_____

_____

_____

Now think about extending yourself some token of love: flowers, chocolates, maybe slippers or a robe. Or perhaps something less tangible, like visiting your favorite museum, or seeing a movie on your next day off, or making time to get out in nature in the coming week. Brainstorm any ideas here.

_____

_____

_____

_____

_____

_____

Yoga for Healing

Not only is yoga great for relaxation and body awareness, it has also been linked to healing emotional pain. This week, why not try it for yourself by doing one of the following?

- Look for a yoga class in your local community. There are beginner classes for new-comers, and even gentle chair yoga for people who need a little extra support. Some studios offer a free try-out class.

- If you can't sign up for a class, find a free yoga lesson on a streaming site that you can follow along with at home.

Your assignment is to simply try a few simple yoga poses with a sense of curiosity and enjoyment, with no obligation to continue if you decide not to. Pay special attention to how you feel before and after. Write about your experience here.

_____

_____

_____

_____

_____

_____

_____

_____

_____

_____

Write about a trip you have always dreamed about taking. Spend some time on the internet daydreaming about going there, or watch a travel show, or check out some books at the library about the location you're interested in. If you have the resources, start planning the trip.

_____

_____

_____

_____

_____

_____

_____

_____

_____

_____

_____

_____

_____

_____

I am learning to
take care of myself more
and more every day.

Social support is important. Do you have at least one person in your life whom you can depend on when the going gets rough? Write about your current support system. If it feels inadequate, write about what seems to be missing. What would you like your support system to look like a year from now?

_____

_____

_____

_____

_____

_____

_____

_____

_____

_____

_____

_____

_____

_____

Building Your Support Network

For this exercise, you are going to make a list of ways you can bolster your social support. Even if it starts with grabbing coffee, you can start slow and nurture new or underserved friendships over time. Perhaps you have people in your life whom you could reach out to and spend more time with. If you have lost touch with friends or family, consider reestablishing contact. Volunteering is a good way to meet other people who may become friends, plus you are helping others, which is a wonderful feeling.

If building relationships seems beyond your ability, you may want to look into your options for group or individual therapy to help with social anxiety. Your health insurer or Employee Assistance Program can help, or check out the Resources section in the back of this journal (page 138).

My options for building friendships:

Ways to meet new people: _____

People I would like to know better: _____

People I have lost touch with: _____

Places I might like to volunteer: _____

Therapy available to me: _____

Acknowledging your blessings can be a good start for self-care and for building a positive mindset. List the things that you are most thankful for in your life and the happiness they bring you. Even a short list can become a foundation to remind yourself of reasons to be appreciative.

Spirituality is a deeply personal journey. When we feel cut off from the greater universe, we can find it hard to make a meaningful connection with ourselves. Write about where you are on your spiritual or religious journey and where you would like to go. Even if you don't consider yourself a spiritual person, write about what greater purpose and meaning you would like to connect with in your life.

The Mindful Way

Sometimes, we are so trapped in thoughts of the future or past that we forget to experience and enjoy what's happening right now. This is where mindfulness can help. At the most basic level, mindfulness means being in the present and observing what we notice without judgment. By doing so, we can more fully participate in the moment.

For example, as I sit here writing this exercise, I observe how my body feels in my chair. I can describe this feeling as comfortable and, once I tune in to it, a bit chilly. It is a cold day, and I have yet to turn on my furnace. I participate in this moment by pulling on a sweater. Now I am better prepared to continue writing. Try this exercise to see whether you can do the same.

1. Find a comfortable position and take several deep breaths. Allow yourself to relax as you settle into your body.

2. Take some time to observe how you feel without attaching meaning or judgment to what comes up. Simply notice any feelings that are present.

3. Next, describe, out loud or in your mind, how you feel.

4. Now think of how you can participate in the moment. Do you need to adjust your environment, move your body, or eliminate distractions?

When you are finished, take action to participate in the present moment in whatever way you can, completing the task at hand, moving on to something else, making yourself more comfortable, or whatever it may take.

What kinds of self-care do you find healing or fulfilling? Cocooning at home with books, hiking in a forest, cooking, exercising at the gym, enjoying some of your favorite foods? What are some ways you can show up for yourself and for your inner child, to acknowledge and support the emotional absence you experienced in the past?

A Week of Self-Care

As you unlearn the old story that your needs are not important, it will become easier to commit to the self-care practices you began exploring earlier. Use this chart to map out a self-care calendar for the next week. It can include healthy coping strategies from page 31, self-care activities you wrote about on the previous page, or anything else you can think of. Commit to doing at least one of these practices each day, or as many as you realistically think you can fit into your weekly schedule.

Try to be specific. For example, rather than saying, "Get eight hours of sleep," you might write, "Be in bed on Sunday night by 10 p.m. so I can get up at 6 a.m." Keep yourself accountable by returning to this page to check off each item after you complete it.

	Self-Care Practice(s)	Completed
DAY 1		
DAY 2		
DAY 3		
DAY 4		
DAY 5		
DAY 6		
DAY 7		

*Owning our story
and loving ourselves
through that process
is the bravest thing
we'll ever do.*

—BRENÉ BROWN

Section 4

Building Self-Love and Self-Esteem

Children need others to listen to them, validate them, and help them see themselves as good, worthy, lovable people. They have no point of reference to see themselves objectively. Even in the absence of put-downs, shaming, or other forms of verbal abuse, a child's positive self-image does not just happen automatically. It requires consistent emotional care.

Without this care, you may have become someone who struggles to really know who you are, what you want in life, or how to value yourself. You may have a tough time giving or receiving love. You marvel at others with healthy self-esteem. The good news is that these are all skills that can be learned beyond childhood. This part of your journal aims to equip you with the right tools you need to start putting healthy self-knowledge into practice. I am going to challenge your current thinking and help you create a path to better self-esteem and self-love.

Connect with the Good Mother

The Good Mother is an archetype as old as time. Warm and loving, she embraces her children and nurtures them to their full potential. She always wants the best for them and has confidence in their abilities. She forgives their mistakes and teaches them to be kind to themselves.

For this exercise you are going to use your imagination to connect with a loving, nurturing presence. You will want to familiarize yourself with the instructions first so you can perform this meditation without needing to read the page. Begin by sitting comfortably where you won't be disturbed or distracted. Take some deep breaths to calm yourself.

Close your eyes, and in your mind's eye, picture yourself walking down a path in a forest. Notice the sunlight filtering through the trees to warm your skin. Walk forward in your mind until you look up and see the path coming to an end. You see the roof of a house up ahead. You decide to check it out.

As you approach, you see a lovely house and get a warm feeling looking at it. You are surprised when a woman says hello from the porch. She has the biggest smile on her face and waves you over. She seems harmless, so you decide to approach.

Her face has gorgeous laugh lines, and she moves like a dancer. Her energy is pure positivity and radiance, and you are drawn to her. She seems to glow with goodness and light. She is so happy to see you! This is the Good Mother.

Give yourself five to ten minutes to approach and spend time with the Good Mother. The wonderful news is, since she exists inside of your imagination, you can visit her whenever you want. The more you visit, the more present she will be.

If you've repressed your longing for a Good Mother, it can be challenging when those feelings reemerge. Thankfully, that longing can be repurposed for your healing now.

After the previous exercise, take some time to make your own representation of the Good Mother. Write a description of what your Good Mother looks like. You may even try creating a collage of her using found images or drawing a picture.

Think of a question to ask your Good Mother. It doesn't have to be profound; something simple will do. Picture her in your mind's eye and see whether she answers you. Write your question and her answer here. When difficulties arise in your life and you need her guidance, see whether you can find a quiet place to return to the house in the woods and talk with her. You can keep a record of this here, too.

_____

_____

_____

_____

_____

_____

_____

_____

_____

_____

_____

_____

_____

_____

After spending time with the Good Mother in the previous prompts, ask yourself how she would nurture you when you need to feel loved. By making you a cup of tea? Playing your favorite music? Running you a warm bath? Now think of how you can turn these into acts of self-care, and list some simple practices you can start today. Use the Good Mother exercise (page 70) if you'd like to ask her for suggestions.

Your Best Traits

Acknowledging our good qualities can be difficult when we lack a foundation—built during childhood by our parents—for doing this. You can help build your feeling of self-worth by truly acknowledging your best traits to yourself.

To begin, use the space below to list your best traits. If you struggle to see your positive traits, imagine the best things that people close to you would list, and write them down. You can list that you are proactive and brave because you are confronting your past and working through this journal.

Now look at the list that you made. Choose one or more of those traits and describe a time in your life when you exhibited that quality.

_____

_____

_____

_____

_____

_____

_____

_____

_____

_____

_____

_____

_____

_____

_____

Write a sentence or two that you would have most wanted to hear as a child from your emotionally absent mother. In what areas of your life did you feel like you needed the most support? Can you visualize how getting the encouragement and reassurance you longed for would have had a positive impact on your life?

Friendly Reminders

An affirmation is a sentence that we can repeat to ourselves to uplift our thoughts and build our ego. Look back at the Your Best Traits exercise (page 74) and turn your strengths into positive affirmations. For example, perhaps you wrote that you are kind. You could write, "I am kind to those around me." Write down five affirmations below.

1. _____

_____

2. _____

_____

3. _____

_____

4. _____

_____

5. _____

_____

Next, copy and post your affirmations someplace where you'll see them frequently. Read them out loud each day to remind yourself of what makes you lovable.

Today I will show
myself love, compassion,
and patience.

Loving yourself includes knowing when to take a break. Write about a time when you could have really used some downtime but pushed yourself instead. How did it feel? What did your body and mind need?

_____

_____

_____

_____

_____

_____

_____

_____

_____

_____

_____

_____

_____

_____

The next time you need a break, how will you take care of yourself? List as many methods as you can think of. You can refer back to the healthy coping strategies on page 31 as a starting point.

_____

_____

_____

_____

_____

_____

_____

_____

_____

_____

_____

_____

_____

_____

_____

_____

Think about a time when you supported a good friend who was going through a rough patch. How did you treat your friend? Were you kind and nonjudgmental? Describe it here.

_____

_____

_____

_____

_____

_____

_____

_____

_____

_____

_____

_____

_____

_____

_____

_____

Now recall a time when you were harsh or unforgiving to yourself. How would you talk to yourself differently if you supported yourself in the same way you encouraged your friend? What positive self-talk comes to mind?

_____

_____

_____

_____

_____

_____

_____

_____

_____

_____

_____

_____

_____

_____

_____

_____

List some ways in which you neglect your own well-being. Do you eat a nourishing diet? Get enough sleep? Attend to your hygiene? What are some ways you are willing to change any unhealthy patterns?

_____

_____

_____

_____

_____

_____

_____

_____

_____

_____

_____

_____

_____

_____

Self-Love Affirmations

The power of meditation is respected and acknowledged throughout the world. Different cultures place different values on meditation, but many cultures acknowledge its usefulness in keeping the brain healthy and the heart and mind aligned. Here's a simple exercise for self-love, based on a meditation by author Kamal Ravikant.

1. Sit comfortably in a quiet place where you won't be disturbed. Set a timer for two minutes.

2. Close your eyes and relax into your seat. Sit alone with your thoughts and focus your attention on your breathing. Notice your lungs filling and emptying as you inhale and exhale.

3. Repeat in your mind, or even say out loud, "I love me" or "I love myself." Continue through several cycles of calm, deep breathing. Finish with a single deep breath, open your eyes, and sit comfortably until you're ready to get up or the two minutes have elapsed.

4. Try repeating this exercise regularly. And, as Ravikant suggests, prior to subjecting yourself to anything negative, ask yourself, "If I love myself, should I make myself do this?"

When is the last time you had fun? What sorts of activities bring you pleasure? How can you incorporate at least one fun thing into your life, as soon as possible?

What about love and joy? Write about when you last felt these emotions. Was it with someone who is close to you, with your pets, or during an outing in nature? Consider how you can cultivate these feelings in your life moving forward.

When you think about receiving love from yourself and from others, what comes up for you? Is there any resistance? Do you allow yourself to feel worthy and deserving of love? Write down the thoughts and feelings that come to mind.

Increasing your spiritual well-being will help you in countless ways. For some, this is related to a higher power; for others, this simply means connecting with a greater purpose or meaning in life. How do you currently nurture your spirit? Reading books? Attending religious services? Learning about the universe beyond our planet? Enjoying the great outdoors? List your methods here, reflect on how they help you, and write about any new ideas you would like to try.

I believe that one defines oneself by reinvention. To not be like your parents. To not be like your friends. To be yourself. To cut yourself out of stone.

—HENRY ROLLINS

Rewriting Your Story

An important aspect of healing from childhood neglect is stepping out of the limited story you replay in your mind. Understanding your mother's experience is an important step in understanding your own. You can develop compassion for your wounded mother and also honor the pain of your wounded inner child. It is time to release any unmet expectations of your mother, let go of negative emotions and patterns from your childhood, and start to write a healthier, positive narrative for yourself.

This section of your journal will help you nurture the supportive relationships you have built and focus on the positives in your life. Always remember, you possess the building blocks necessary to construct a healthier life.

Near the start of this journal, you wrote about your mother's story (page 3). Now that you've had some time to work through your memories and feelings, return to that exercise and see whether you have a clearer picture of her story. Did she herself struggle to be loved as a child, perhaps in the same ways you did? What was going on for her as you were growing up? How did she struggle with motherhood? What regrets might she express about her life?

What does compassion for your wounded mother look like to you? Finding compassion doesn't mean letting her continue to hurt you. Forgiveness and reconciliation are two different things. Forgiveness, as theology and ethics professor Lewis B. Smedes wrote, occurs when "we set a prisoner free and discover that the prisoner we set free is us." Forgiveness is a solo act that we do for ourselves so we can let go of a grudge and move forward. Reconciliation involves building trust again with the offender, which may not be possible or advisable, since reconciling with someone who is still hurting us is not being kind to ourselves. Perhaps your expectations of your mother can change. Perhaps you are not ready to forgive. Either way, finding some compassion for your mother can help you heal. What would this look like?

_____

_____

_____

_____

_____

_____

_____

_____

_____

_____

_____

There comes a time when we must stop holding on to the hope that our mother can meet certain expectations. What expectations do you need to let go of? Are you still hoping she will become someone she is not capable of becoming? Given what you know about your mother, and assuming she is not going to change significantly, what would a realistic expectation look like?

A Letter for Your Mother

For this exercise you are going to write a letter to your mother. This is not for her eyes; it is only for you. Use the previous prompts to construct a new narrative—one where you are on the path to being whole and healed and understand your mother's limitations. Write about how you feel now and what has changed. Even if you do not feel healed yet, use this letter to release any resentment or bitterness you may feel.

EXERCISE CONTINUED →

What unhelpful tendencies or patterns from childhood are you still holding on to? Do you find it hard to ask for help, for example? Is it difficult to take care of yourself, make friends, or open up romantically? You might want to refer back to the prompts about attachment styles on pages 24 to 28 to think about behaviors you would like to change.

Write about how you would like to develop new ways of being. Feel free to include any insight you've gained or tools you've learned about in this journal.

Know Your Own Strength

Rewriting your story includes taking stock of the strengths you developed because of your childhood. For those who have come through emotional neglect, these tend to include the attributes listed below. Check any that apply to you.

I am:

☐ A good listener

☐ A diligent worker

☐ A compassionate friend

☐ Loyal to others

☐ Self-reflective

☐ Responsible

☐ Persistent

☐ Brave

List any other strengths you can think of:

_____

_____

_____

_____

_____

_____

_____

_____

Now select the strength you admire the most in yourself. How has it helped you up to now, and how can it continue to help you in the future?

I hold the power to define my own story.

Imagine you could speak to yourself as a child and give a fuller picture of what happened during your childhood rather than the restricted, self-blaming story you believed then. Write down what you would say to explain things to your younger self. If you wish, you can also try doing this off the page, by returning to the exercise Connect with Your Younger Self on page 19.

How can you speak the truth of your story, sharing the experiences of your childhood and how it has impacted your life? Reflect on how you can express your truth to yourself, to loved ones, to a therapist. List any people who you feel will be supportive, and write about what you would like to share with them. Remember, it's important to find those who can extend understanding and empathy, rather than those who may dismiss or minimize what you went through (page 35).

Write about a different decision you could have made in your life, one that would have been made by someone with a more positive self-image. Perhaps you would have applied to different schools, tried out for a team, or asked for a raise at work. How can you create some of that different result now, in your current life?

_____

_____

_____

_____

_____

_____

_____

_____

_____

_____

_____

_____

_____

Flip the Script

Now that you have gained greater self-compassion and put parts of your past into perspective, correct the following unhealthy, negative statements with more helpful beliefs about yourself. There is space to add your own negative statements to reframe at the end of this exercise, too.

Negative: I should care for others more than myself.

Positive: When I take care of myself, I'm able to take care of others.

Negative: My past limits my future.

Positive: _____

Negative: Self-worth comes from what others think about me.

Positive: _____

Negative: Deep down, I am flawed.

Positive: _____

Negative: It is risky to rely on others for help.

Positive: _____

Negative: I am hard on myself.

Positive: _____

Negative: It's safer to keep my feelings to myself.

Positive: _____

Negative: A happier future is beyond my reach.

Positive: _____

Negative: _____

Positive: _____

Negative: _____

Positive: _____

Negative: _____

Positive: _____

Take a few minutes to imagine your life ten years from now. Write about what becomes possible for you as you find healing from the past and integrate self-compassion and self-care into your life.

_____

_____

_____

_____

_____

_____

_____

_____

_____

_____

_____

_____

_____

_____

A Vision Board

Visualization is a powerful practice. When you spend time focusing on what you want in your life, you become more oriented to it and can better organize your behavior around it. One way to visualize is to make a vision board.

A vision board is a collection of images of what you want in your life. Making one provides you with a visual reminder of what your dreams, desires, plans, and goals for the future are. It can help you stay on track, feel inspired, and feel connected to yourself.

1. To create one, gather magazines, catalogs, printed images from the internet, and any other sources of words and images available.

2. Cut out words and images that inspire you or relate to your goals. Write out aspirations and favorite quotes.

3. Tape, glue, or pin words and images onto a sheet of paper, poster board, or bulletin board. Let your creativity flow, and see where it takes you.

4. When you finish, post your vision board somewhere in your home where you can look at it for daily inspiration.

How can you commit to taking responsibility for yourself and making sure you're treated fairly? This may mean advocating for yourself at work, with a partner, or with a friend. It may look like listening to your body when you feel tired, or to your mind when you feel overwhelmed.

How will life feel when you are able to consistently speak kindly to yourself and prioritize your mental, physical, emotional, and spiritual needs? What will that look like?

A Letter from Your Future Self

Write a letter from your future self to your current self. Tell yourself about all the work you have done, any things you have stopped or started doing, and what your goals are. Be open and honest.

_____

_____

_____

_____

_____

_____

_____

_____

_____

_____

_____

_____

_____

_____

As you process the past and move toward healing, your story changes. Do you see your life differently now than you did when you began this journal? In what ways are you able to see your relationship with your mother more objectively?

_____

_____

_____

_____

_____

_____

_____

_____

_____

_____

_____

_____

_____

_____

_____

_____

_____

How can you reframe your story to help you take responsibility to be a mother to yourself and accept support from others now and into the future?

_____

_____

_____

_____

_____

_____

_____

_____

_____

_____

_____

_____

_____

_____

We must rewrite our story from one of fear to one of celebration.

—KAMERON HURLEY

Section 6

Continuing Your Healing Journey

Congratulations! You are one section away from completing this journal. Of course, your healing journey will continue beyond the final page, and there is no fixed timeline or trajectory for your progress. It may sometimes be a difficult path to follow, but take heart that you are putting in the effort to move toward a brighter future.

As you continue this process, don't be alarmed if it sometimes seems like you have taken a step forward and then a step back. You are a work in progress, and this work is not easy. My hope is that you will use what you have learned about yourself in this journal to chart a better path forward.

This journal has been its own journey of self-discovery. What have you learned about yourself? List something positive relating to your past, present, and future.

My past:

_____

_____

_____

_____

My present:

_____

_____

_____

_____

My future:

_____

_____

_____

_____

As we explored earlier in this journal (pages 24 to 28), our early experiences influence our attachment styles, which greatly affect how we relate to the people around us. Now that you have more insight into how you form relationships, reflect on how you can forge healthier bonds with those around you. If you have traits of anxious attachment, write about what it would look like to better value yourself in relationships, prioritize your needs, and advocate for yourself. If you have traits of avoidant attachment, how can healing past hurt free you to be more vulnerable and to drop defenses that keep others at arm's length?

What do you have to look forward to on your healing journey? Perhaps you will take better care of yourself, travel to new places, or go back to school. Pick one or more benefits awaiting you and write about them.

_____

_____

_____

_____

_____

_____

_____

_____

_____

_____

_____

_____

_____

_____

Expressing Gratitude

Learning to find gratitude in our everyday experiences helps us as we grow and come to accept the lessons along our journey. Fostering a gratitude practice is a simple yet powerful way to transform your perspective on life—helping you to become more aware of what you have, rather than what you lack.

Start by making a list of three things that you feel grateful for right now. These might be something simple, like the first cup of coffee of the day, or more significant, like the support of your friends or the strides you have made in learning to look after yourself.

1. _____

2. _____

3. _____

Moving forward, try making this a daily practice. You can keep a written journal that you add to before you go to sleep at night or a digital document on your phone that you add to throughout the day. Start each day by reading your gratitude journal. With time, finding reasons to feel grateful will become easier and easier.

If you are a parent or want children in the future, it's important to remember that you can provide the emotional support that you yourself lacked. Write about the ways you can be emotionally available to your actual or future children. In what ways can you be compassionate and open with them? If you do not see yourself having children, you can write about other young people in your life, like nieces, nephews, or the kids of close friends.

Permission to Feel

After growing up in a home where you lacked a model for coping with fear, sadness, shame, anger, and other difficult emotions, you may still find yourself turning to unhealthy coping strategies (page 32) when these feelings arise. The truth is, even though your healing will reduce the frequency and intensity of these emotions, they are impossible for anyone to avoid altogether. They are a natural part of life.

A key part of your long-term well-being will be learning not to fight, control, or escape strong feelings whenever they appear, but to be more accepting of them. You can allow them to come and go without acting on them immediately. The next time you notice a challenging emotion, try practicing the following steps:

1. Step back, name the emotion, and observe it.

2. Let go of judgments about the emotion.

3. Notice your body sensations.

4. Practice being willing to accept the emotion and the sensations it brings.

5. Visualize the emotion as a cloud moving across the sky, floating away and out of view.

6. Notice any unhealthy coping urges you might have, without acting on them.

7. Remind yourself of times when you have not felt this emotion.

8. Say to yourself, "I accept this emotion."

Afterward, notice how you feel. Sometimes when we stay with a feeling, another one makes itself heard. Return to this practice as often as you can.

I have come so far on my journey. I am excited to see what the future holds.

We can't change the past, but we can improve our present and our future. Learning to accept the past, rather than feeling trapped by the confusion, hurt, or disappointment our younger self felt, can free us to lead a more fulfilling life. Now that you can make better sense of what you've been through, write about what acceptance of your past looks and feels like.

How are you already able to become the Good Mother (pages 70 to 73) to your inner child? How would you like to do so in the future?

_____

_____

_____

_____

_____

_____

_____

_____

_____

_____

_____

_____

_____

_____

_____

In the past you may have put others' needs before your own, found it hard to say no, and agreed with others to avoid conflict. Looking ahead, describe ways that you can challenge this thinking. What boundaries would you like to set with others that you were not able to before? How will this improve your life?

_____

_____

_____

_____

_____

_____

_____

_____

_____

_____

_____

_____

_____

_____

Improving Your Relationships

The attachment style we learn in childhood continue to act as a model for our relationships into adulthood. Whether you find yourself anxious how others feel about you in relationships or avoid getting close to others (or have a mix of the two styles), the following inventory will give you a chance to identify the things you currently do well and the areas you'd like to improve.

Put a check for the items you already do well and a plus symbol for the skills you want to improve, be it with friends, a romantic partner, or anyone else.

☐ Communicating my feelings, needs, or desires

☐ Knowing how to protect my time, emotional energy, or physical comfort or safety

☐ Taking the lead in a relationship

☐ Soothing my partner

☐ Detecting early on when people I care about are upset in a conversation

☐ De-escalating stressful interactions

☐ Keeping a conversation on topic during conflict

☐ Showing appreciation and gratitude

☐ Seeking support from loved ones when I need it

☐ Collaborating for a win-win

☐ Opening up to and trusting others

Each of these is an important skill for promoting security in close relationships. If there are any other areas of your relationships you would like to improve, write them down below.

_____

_____

_____

_____

Now, for the items on the previous page you want to work on, what are ways you can think of to improve? If nothing comes to mind, you can draw inspiration from something you've already learned in this journal, look for more information in the Resources on page 138, or talk about ideas with somebody you have a mutually trusting and respectful relationship with, such as a partner, close friend, or therapist.

A Letter from Your Mother

In this final letter-writing exercise, pen a short letter to yourself from your mother. Use this as a space to express what has been unsaid and to find more closure. Imagine what she might say to you if she were speaking honestly and compassionately. What might she say about your relationship, her mistakes, and what she hopes for your future?

Growing up, you likely learned to be self-reliant and take care of your own needs. As you heal, you will find it easier to reach out to others without feeling needy or ashamed. Use the space below to brainstorm ways to foster this. Perhaps it's confiding more openly in your partner, reaching out to friends in times of need, finding an online or in-person support group, speaking with a therapist (see the Resources, page 138), or finding an accountability partner who will encourage you to follow through as you take on healthy coping strategies.

Consider the role of social connection in your healing. Humans are by design social creatures with a need for belonging and community. How is this need met currently in your life? How could you make time to spend with others socially and connect with people in a meaningful way? Feel free to brainstorm ideas, like taking a music class, joining a sports club, or anything that comes to mind.

Life presents us with countless opportunities. When we have an opportunity to do something, we can say yes or no. Sometimes we say no because we think we might fail. We don't even give ourselves the chance to try. When was the last time you said no to an opportunity because you feared that you would fail? How can you use this reflection to say yes next time?

_____

_____

_____

_____

_____

_____

_____

_____

_____

_____

_____

_____

_____

_____

_____

How would you describe your relationship with yourself now that you've worked through this journal? What has changed? What have you strengthened?

What does long-term self-care look like to you? How will you know you are on the right path? Describe your self-care goals for the following milestones.

A month from now:

_____

_____

_____

_____

A year from now:

_____

_____

_____

_____

Ten years from now:

_____

_____

_____

_____

Take a moment to breathe in the accomplishment of completing this journal. What comes up for you emotionally? List one or two messages that you would like to offer yourself regarding this courageous endeavor.

_____

_____

_____

_____

_____

_____

_____

_____

_____

_____

_____

_____

_____

_____

_____

A Final Word

Congratulations! You have come to the end of this journal. This is no small feat, and you can be proud of yourself for doing this difficult yet important work. Of course, your healing journey may not end here. You may find yourself encountering certain issues you've explored for some time to come. However, once seen, the truth cannot be unseen. My hope is that in acknowledging the reality of your past—and coming closer to a place of acceptance—you have gained a degree of liberation that can continue to heal you for years to come.

I encourage you to continue the self-care and self-love practices you have developed. As you move ahead, you may want to add your own. You will find these practices easier and more natural the more you do them. In the Resources on the following pages, you will find additional materials you can explore to continue your journey.

The process of growth is not always linear. Some days will be harder than others, and certain unhelpful self-beliefs may take longer to change, but be patient with yourself and take heart in the progress you make. Giving yourself the compassion and care you lacked in childhood will pay dividends in every area of your life. My hope is that you continue to be kind to yourself along the way.

Resources

Finding a Therapist

Give an Hour, free therapy for active-duty military, veterans, and their family members: GiveAnHour.org.

Good Therapy, mental health information clearinghouse and therapist search tool: GoodTherapy.org.

Open Path, sliding scale counseling: OpenPathCollective.org.

Psychology Today, therapist search tool: PsychologyToday.com/us/therapists.

Meditation Resources

There are many great resources available to help you practice mindfulness and meditate, even for beginners. You can find free guided meditations on video and music streaming sites or on podcasts. Or you can try downloading an app for your smartphone, such as Calm, Breathe, or Headspace. Find what works for you and try to make it a part of your daily or weekly routine. Even five or ten minutes a day can help foster a sense of calm and balance.

Books

Brown, Nina. *Children of the Self-Absorbed: A Grown-Up's Guide to Getting over Narcissistic Parents*. New Harbinger Publications, third edition, April 2020.

Forward, Susan. *Mothers Who Can't Love: A Healing Guide for Daughters*. Harper Paperbacks, October 2014.

McBride, Karyl. *Will I Ever Be Good Enough? Healing the Daughters of Narcissistic Mothers*. Free Press, September 2008.

Miller, Alice. *The Drama of the Gifted Child: The Search for the True Self.* Basic Books, revised, updated edition, July 2008.

Ravikant, Kamal. *Love Yourself like Your Life Depends on It*. HarperOne, January 2020.

Stephens, Brenda. *Recovering from Narcissistic Mothers: A Daughter's Guide*. Rockridge Press, January 2021.

Van der Kolk, Bessel. *The Body Keeps the Score: Brain, Mind, and Body in the Healing of Trauma*. Viking, September 2014.

Wiest, Brianna. *The Mountain Is You: Transforming Self-Sabotage into Self-Mastery*. Thought Catalog Books, May 2020.

References

Bowlby, John. *Attachment and Loss*, vol. 1, *Attachment*. 1st ed. London: Penguin Books, 1971.

Bowlby, John. *Child Care and the Growth of Love*. London: Penguin Books, 1953. Version of WHO publication *Maternal Care and Mental Health* published for sale to the general public.

Howes, Ryan. "Forgiveness vs. Reconciliation." *Psychology Today*, March 31, 2013. PsychologyToday.com/us/blog/in-therapy/201303/forgiveness-vs-reconciliation.

Ravikant, Kamal. *Love Yourself like Your Life Depends on It*. San Francisco: HarperOne, 2020.

Smedes, Lewis B. *Forgive and Forget: Healing the Hurts We Don't Deserve*. San Francisco: HarperOne, 2007.

Acknowledgments

To my husband, Jim. You've always said I should write a book. Thank you for believing in me. To my oldest friend, Loucile. I could not have done this without you. To my son, Charlie. You make it all worthwhile.

About the Author

CHRISTY LINCOLN, MA, LCPC, specializes in working with adults who have experienced childhood abuse and neglect. She has worked in many clinical settings, including her private practice, for over 20 years. She teaches psychology at Sauk Valley Community College and Southern New Hampshire University. A zoologist at heart, she lives in rural Illinois with her family.

CPSIA information can be obtained
at www.ICGtesting.com
Printed in the USA
JSHW012026180422
24991JS00003B/5